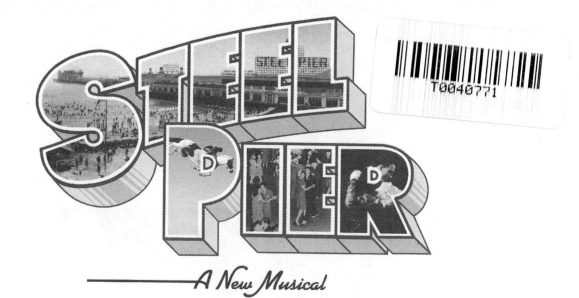

STEEL PIER

A New Musical

Lyrics by
FRED EBB

Music by
JOHN KANDER

Editing by David Loud
Vocal Selections prepared by Paul McKibbins

ISBN 0-634-08477-1

HAL•LEONARD®
CORPORATION
7777 W. BLUEMOUND RD. P.O. BOX 13819 MILWAUKEE, WI 53213

Visit Hal Leonard Online at
www.halleonard.com

John Kander & Fred Ebb

Theatre: *Flora, the Red Menace; Cabaret; The Happy Time; Zorba; Chicago; 70, Girls, 70; The Act; Woman of the Year; The Rink; And the World Goes 'Round—The Kander & Ebb Musical; Kiss of the Spider Woman.* Films: *Cabaret; Lucky Lady; NY, NY; Funny Lady; Kramer vs. Kramer; A Matter of Time; Places in the Heart; French Postcards; Stepping Out.* Television: "Liza with a Z" (Liza Minnelli), "Goldie and Liza Together" (With Goldie Hawn), "Ol' Blue Eyes Is Back," "Baryshnikov on Broadway," "An Early Frost," "Liza in London." Upcoming: *The Skin of Our Teeth.*

CONTENTS

RITA'S THEME

Words by FRED EBB
Music by JOHN KANDER

Moderately

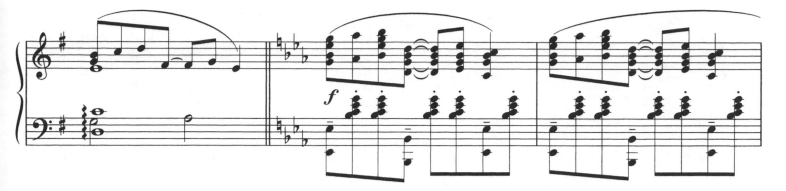

WILLING TO RIDE

Words by FRED EBB
Music by JOHN KANDER

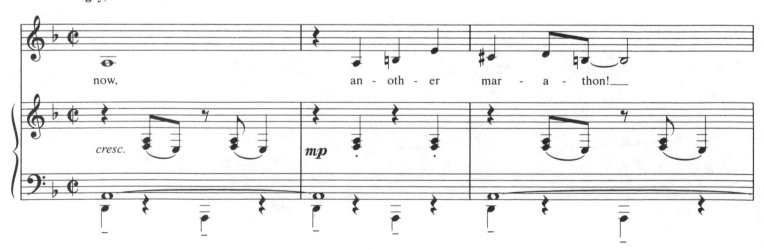

8

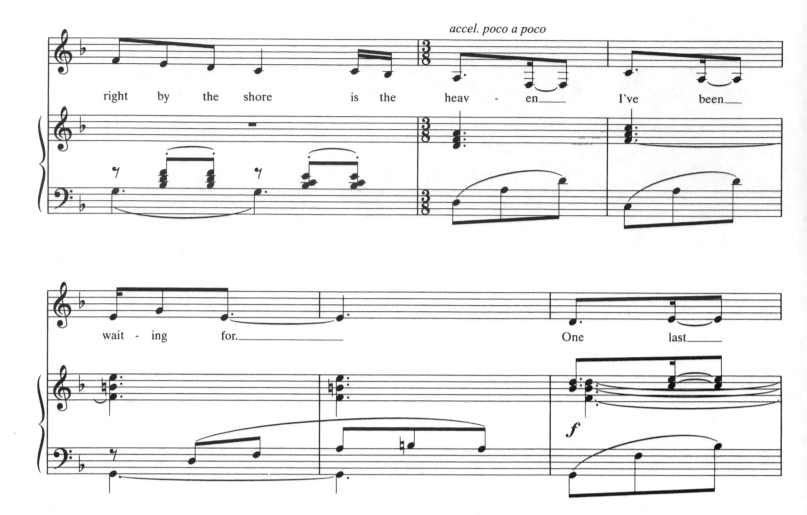

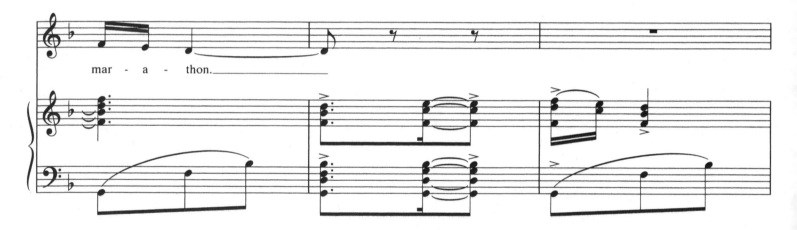

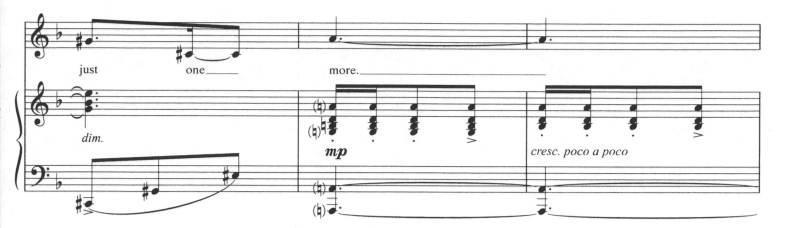

just one____ more._____

dim.

mp

cresc. poco a poco

poco rit.

Tempo I

Here I go a -

mf

gain. I can hear that mer - ry - go - round, and

though I nev - er cared much for the sound, I'm will - ing to ride._____

cresc.

There's the fer - ris wheel,_____ a

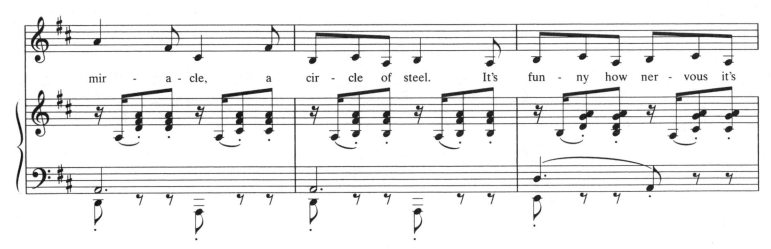

mir - a - cle, a cir - cle of steel. It's fun - ny how ner - vous it's

mak - ing me feel, yet will - ing to ride._____

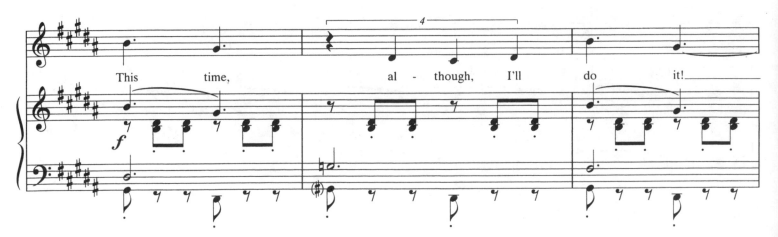

This time, al - though, I'll do it!_____

I swear it's the last time_____ I'll ev - er

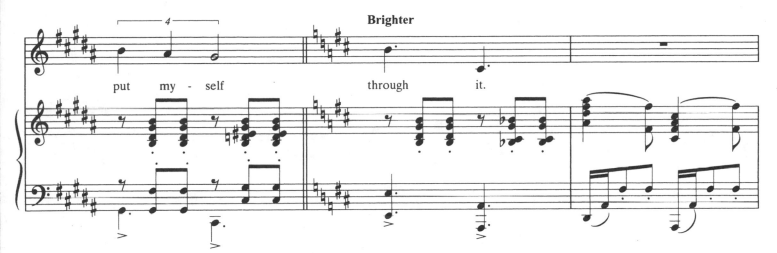

Brighter

put my - self through it.

I have to stop re - mem - ber - ing when, and

now must be now, and then must be then. I'm learn - ing to qui - et that

rall.

but - ter - fly ri - ot in - side.

I'm will - ing to

A Tempo
(Instrumental)

ride.

ff

(Sung)

But now must be now and then must be then. I've

mf

struck out be - fore and I could - n't for - get if I tried.

But I'm up to bat a - gain,_____ toss - ing my

cresc. poco a poco

hat a - gain._____ Here I go a - gain,_____

a tempo

will - ing to ride._____

a tempo
ff

sfz

SECOND CHANCE

Words by FRED EBB
Music by JOHN KANDER

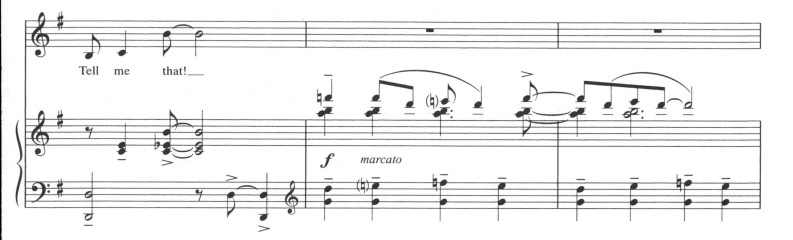

Tell me that!

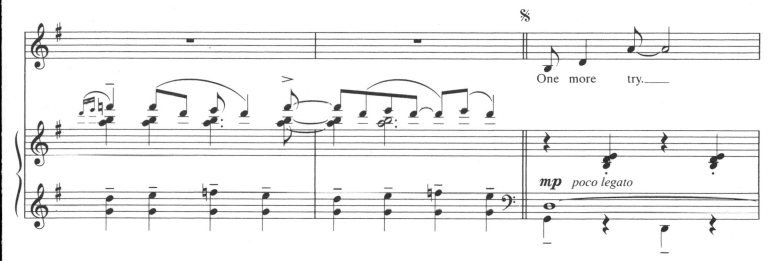

One more try.

Who - ev - er gets to get an - oth - er try?_ Who - ev - er gets to sing the

big re - prise?_ Tell me, please._ Once_ you're down, You're

down, they say.____ Once___ you're out, you're

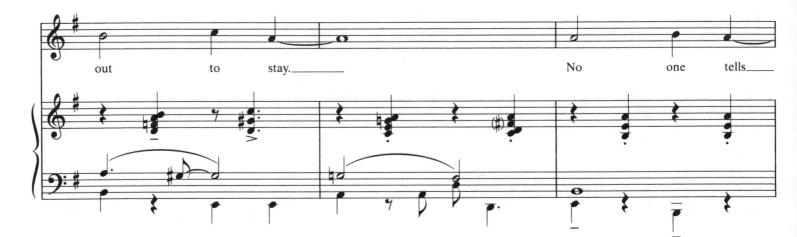

out to stay.____ No one tells____

___ you you can get right__ up and you can start all

o - ver with a sec - ond chance._ When - ev - er life has gone from

bad to worse,___ you've got to run your mov - ie in re - verse.___

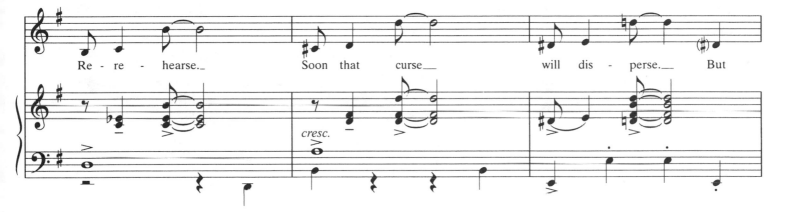

Re - re - hearse.___ Soon that curse___ will dis - perse.___ But

cresc.

To Coda ⊕

first you've got to get_____

f

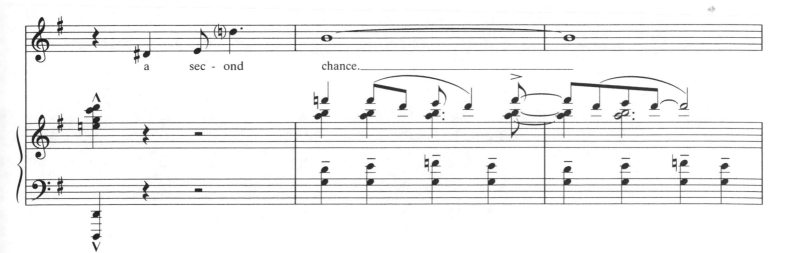

a sec - ond chance._____

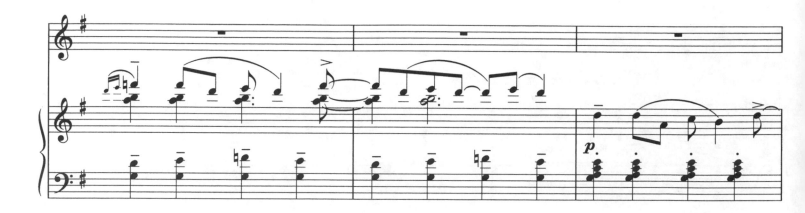

D.S. 𝄋 al Coda

⊕ Coda

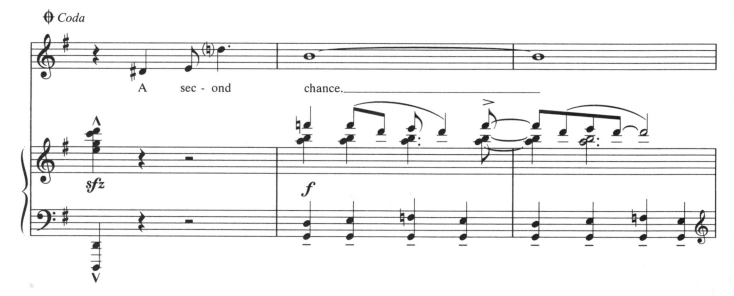

A sec - ond chance.

DANCE WITH ME

Words by FRED EBB
Music by JOHN KANDER

With motion

Dance with me, Dance with me.

Hold me as we cross the floor._____

20

Light as air, what a pair!

Tell me could heav - en be an - y - thing more?_____

cresc.

Whirl a - round, twirl a - round, fol - low me and

mf

soon you'll see_____ Fred and A - dele_____ nev - er

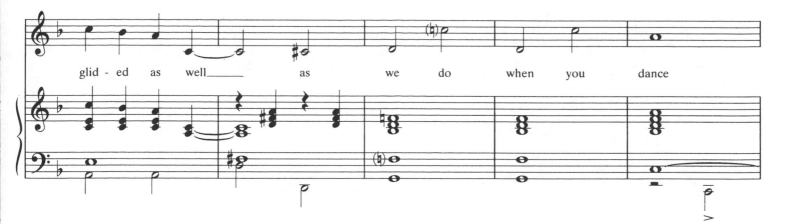

glid - ed as well____ as we do when you dance

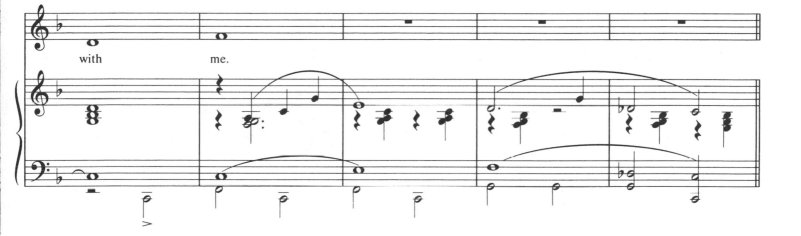

with me.

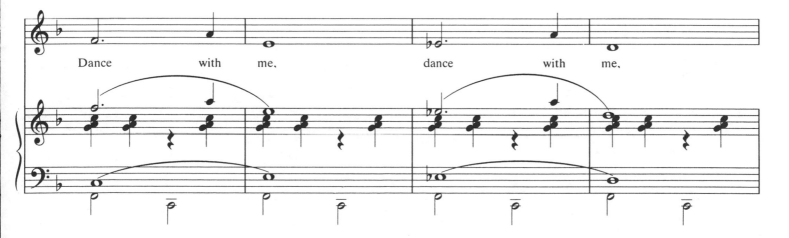

Dance with me, dance with me,

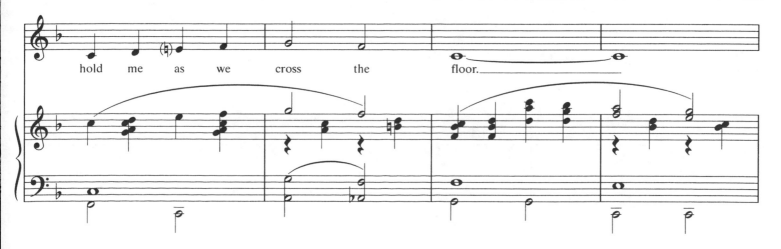

hold me as we cross the floor.____

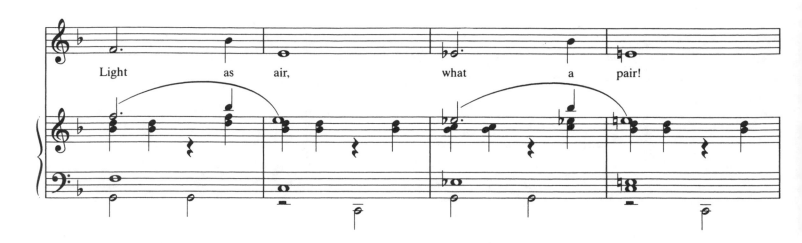

Light as air, what a pair!

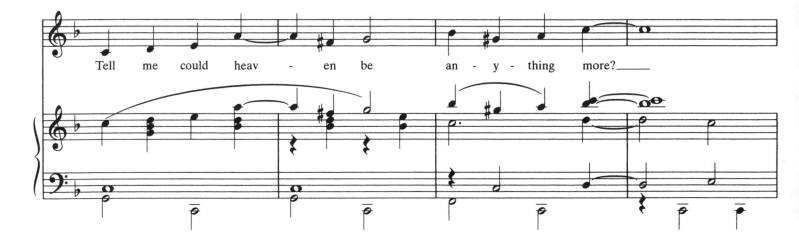

Tell me could heav - en be an - y - thing more?_____

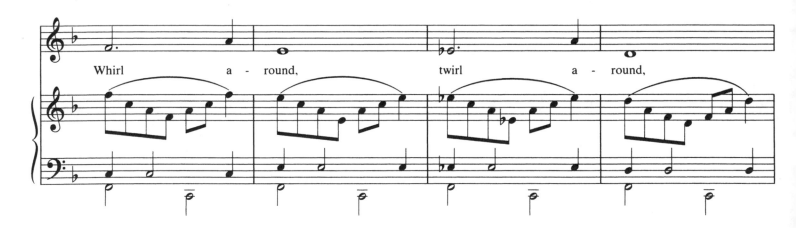

Whirl a - round, twirl a - round,

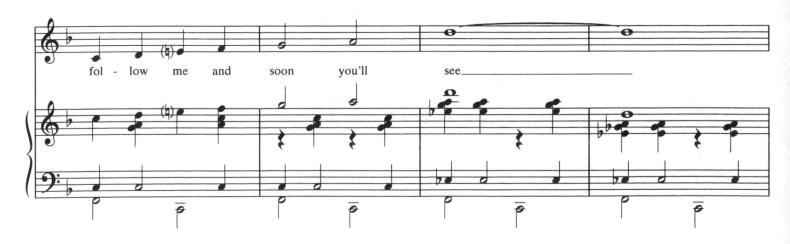

fol - low me and soon you'll see_____

23

Fred and A - dele_____ nev - er glid - ed as well_____ as

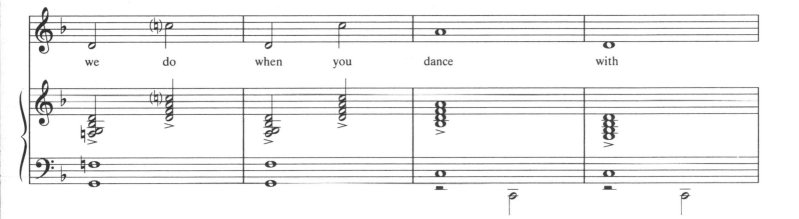

we do when you dance with

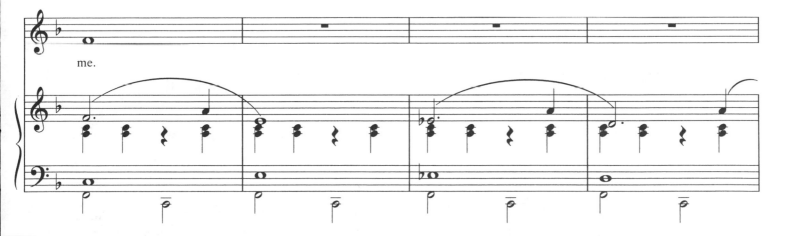

me.

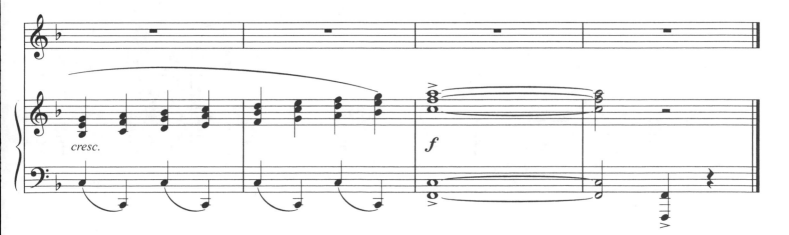

cresc.

f

THE LAST GIRL

Words by FRED EBB
Music by JOHN KANDER

25

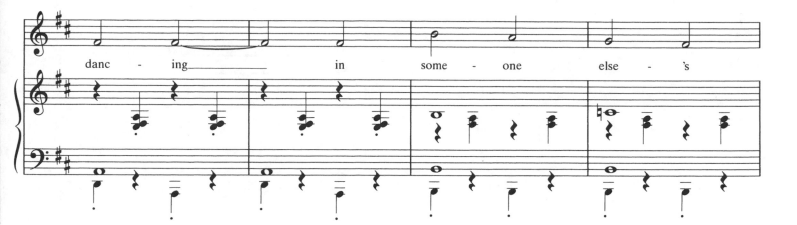

danc - ing _____ in some - one else - 's

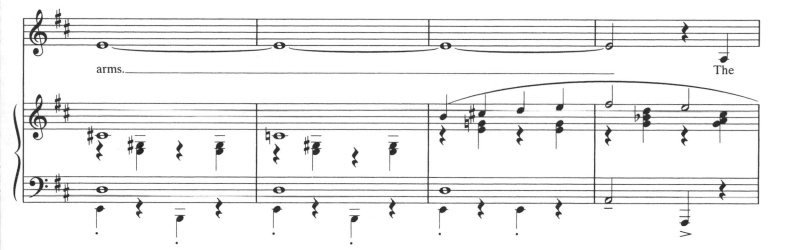

arms. _____ The

last girl _____ I'll care a - bout is

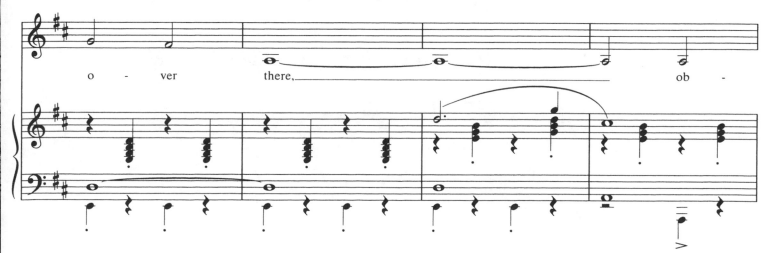

o - ver there, _____ ob -

li - vi - ous, it's clear, _____ of

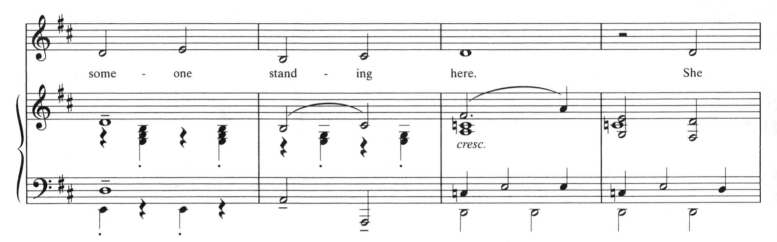

some - one stand - ing here. She

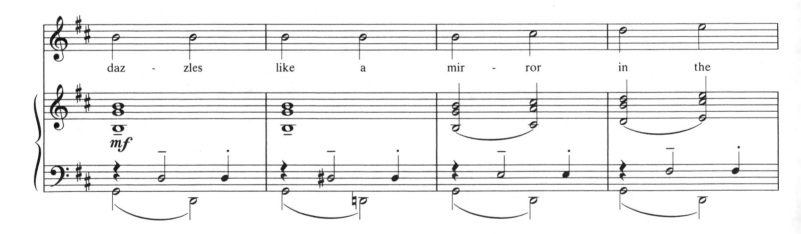

daz - zles like a mir - ror in the

sun. _____ She

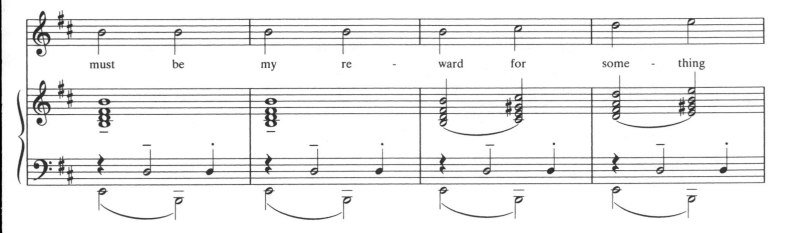

must be my re - ward for some - thing

won - der - ful I've done. The

last girl_____ I'll ev - er love walked

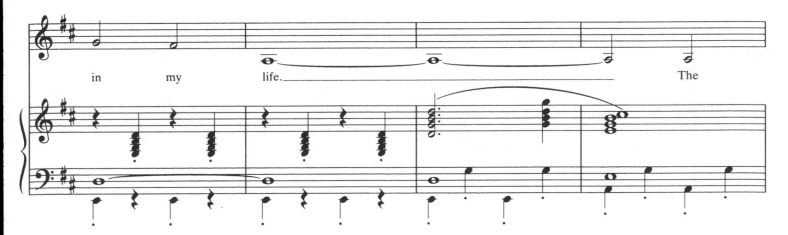

in my life._____ The

mo - ment_____ was strict - ly un - re -

hearsed._____ But The

cresc.

rall. poco a poco

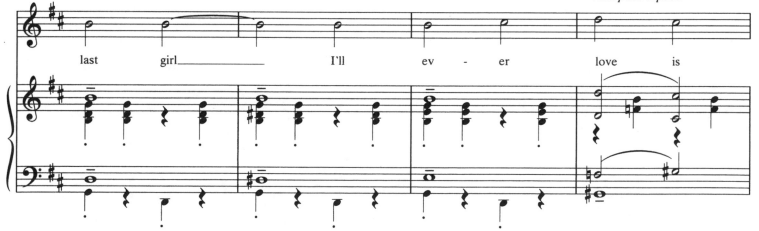

last girl_____ I'll ev - er love is

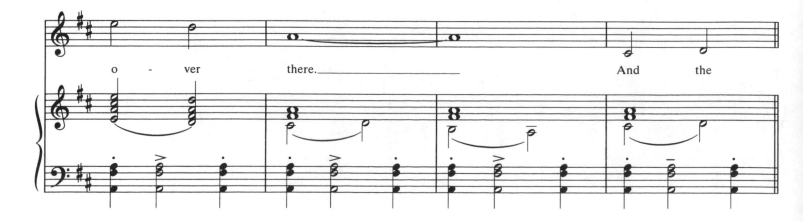

o - ver there._____ And the

A bit slower

last girl,_____ it's a - maz - ing!_____ The last girl,_____

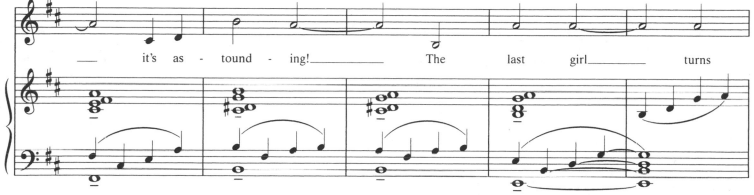

____ it's as - tound - ing!_____ The last girl_____ turns

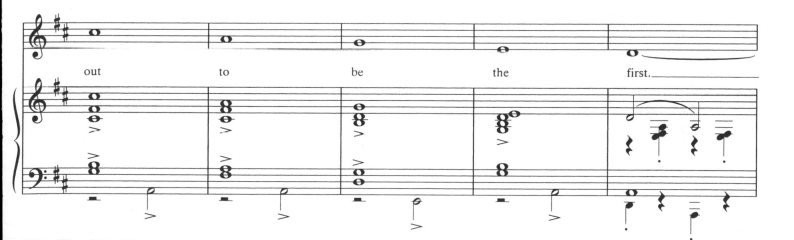

out to be the first._____

EVERYBODY'S GIRL

Words by FRED EBB
Music by JOHN KANDER

Bright tango

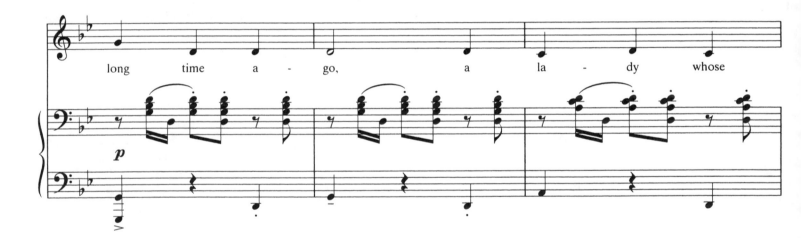

long time a - go, a la - dy whose

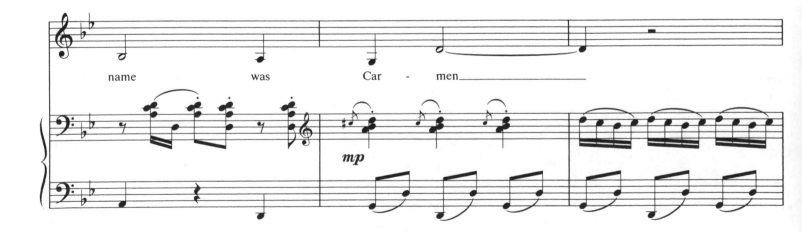

name was Car - men

31

drove a man

wild un - til he was out of con -

trol.

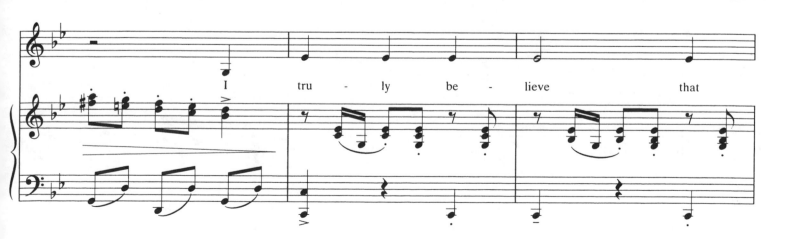

I tru - ly be - lieve that

32

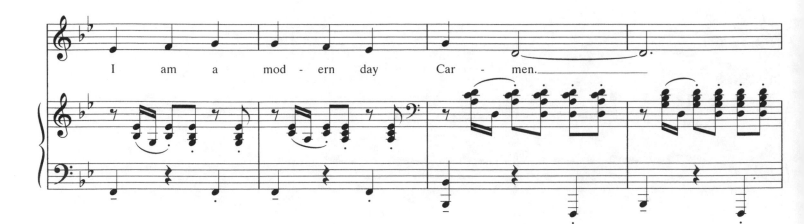

Poco rubato

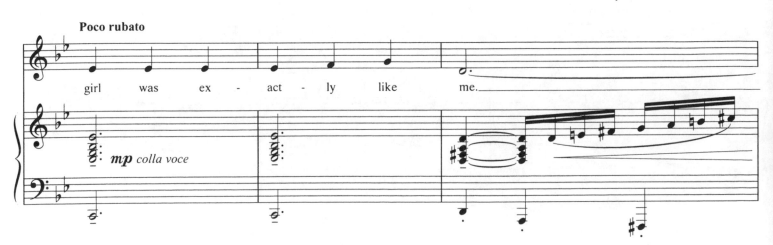

Con poco moto

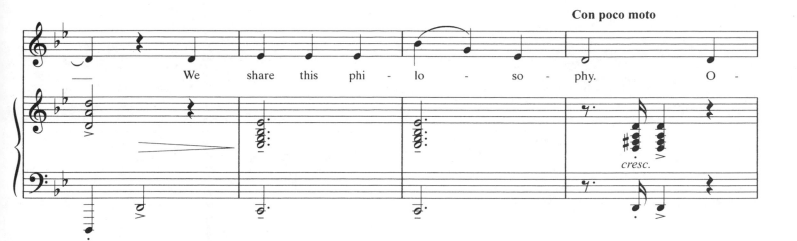

We share this phi - lo - so - phy. O -

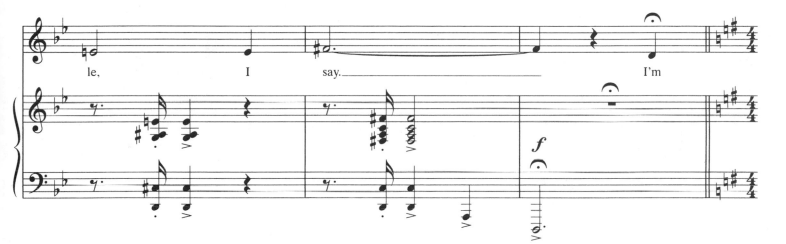

le, I say. I'm

not the type who's read-y for dat - in' some-one stead-y. I'm ev-'ry-bod-y's girl.

mp poco marcato

On Sun-day night, it's Dan-ny, on Mon-day, may-be Man-ny. I'm

ev - 'ry-bod-y's girl._____ There's a point to my be-

hav - ior which is: smart girls al - ways share their rich - es._____

So if your heart suc-cumbs don't let it,____ you're cer - tain to re-gret it.____ All

oth - ers,____ come and get it!_____ I'm ev - 'ry - bod-y's girl.____

With more kick

(Spoken:) I could never be a cowhand's girl.

(Sung:) La la la la la la.

(Spoken:) And do you wanna know why?

ENSEMBLE: Why?

SHELBY: *(Spoken:)* 'Cause I just can't keep my calves together. *(Sung:)* I'm ev-'ry-bod-y's girl.

Some old Greek called A-ri-sto-tle said it:

If you got it, why not spread it?_____ So don't go

rat - tling an - y sa - bres,___ ex - ert - ing an - y la - bors,___ just share me___ with the neigh - bors!____

I'm ev - 'ry - bod - y's girl.____

In

(Spoken:) (Sung:) (Silent:) (Sung:)

case your pas - sion rag - es,___ I'm in the yel - low pag - es I'm (ev - 'ry-bod-y's) girl.___

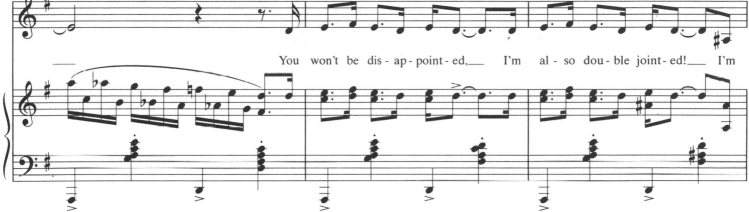

You won't be dis - ap - point - ed,___ I'm al - so dou - ble joint - ed!___ I'm

ev - 'ry-bod-y's girl. Though it leaves a lot of

fel - las curs - in', I'm a per - son needs dis - bur - sin'.___

And so to re-af-firm my sta-tus,___ it's ab-sol-ut-ly grat-is___ to

use my___ ap-par-a-tus.___ I'm ev-ry-bod-y's girl.___

(Spoken:) Men and me are like pianos:
When they get upright, I feel grand.

Ev - 'ry -

bod - y's___ girl.___

(slide)

WET

Words by FRED EBB
Music by JOHN KANDER

Think of all the plea-sure you'll get____ when you're

all   wet.   Not a trou-ble you can't for-get____ when you're

all   wet.   Some folks say that be-ing hap-py is

40

hav - ing bar - rels of cash. But I be - lieve that be - ing hap - py is

here a splash. There a splash.

Let's get rea - dy, set, and be - gin___ to be all wet.

Feel that wa - ter lap - ping your skin___ when you're all wet. Come

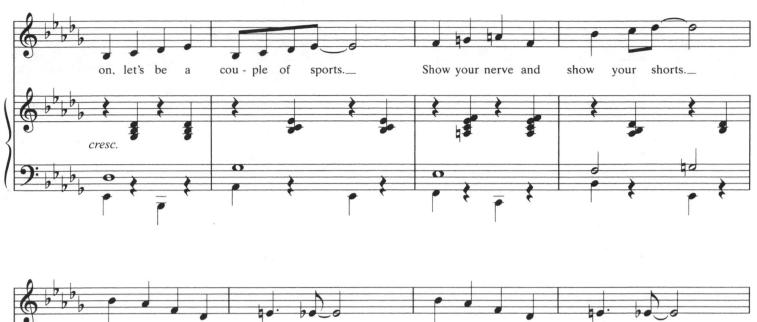

on, let's be a cou - ple of sports.__ Show your nerve and show your shorts.__

There's no time for jok - ing.__ This night could be smok - ing__

once we both get soak - in' wet.

Pa - pa nev - er taught me to swim.____

Think of all the plea - sure you'll get____ when you're all wet.

So right now I'm fum - ing at him.____

Not a trou - ble you can't for - get____ when you're all wet.

start to go down,___ in her arms, a

all wet. Feel that wa - ter lap - ping your skin__ when you're

sim.

nice way to drown.__ All right here I go,

all wet. Come on, let's be a cou - ple of sports._

watch out down be - low.__ All the rules are bro - ken__

Show your nerve and show your shorts._ All the rules are bro - ken__

when the fire is smok - in'.___ Douse it get - ting soak - in'

cresc.

wet.

wet.

8va - loco

Come

Come

8va - loco

46

LOVEBIRD

Words by FRED EBB
Music by JOHN KANDER

Moderately slow
Poco rubato

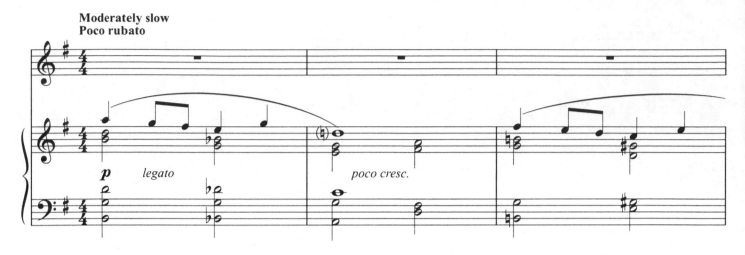

Easy foxtrot

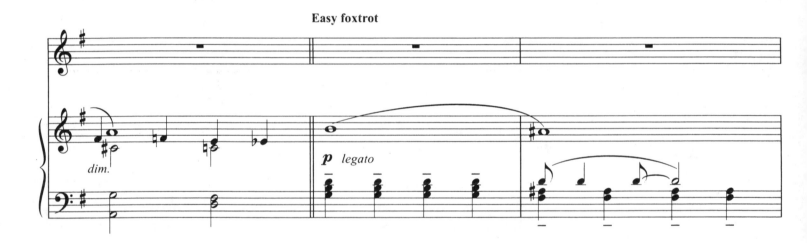

49

feel - ing blue.___ Love - bird, we should be two.___

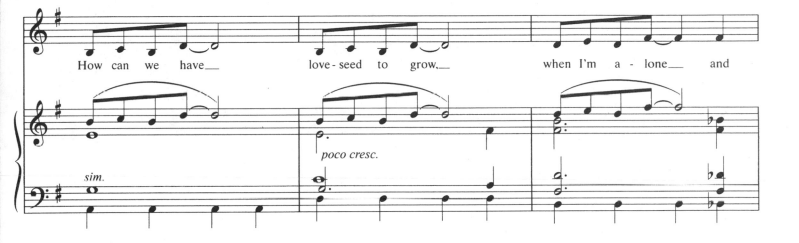

How can we have___ love - seed to grow, when I'm a - lone___ and

poco cresc.

sim.

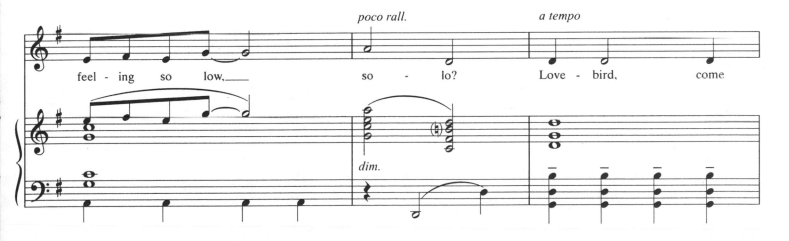

poco rall. *a tempo*

feel - ing so low,___ so - lo? Love - bird, come

dim.

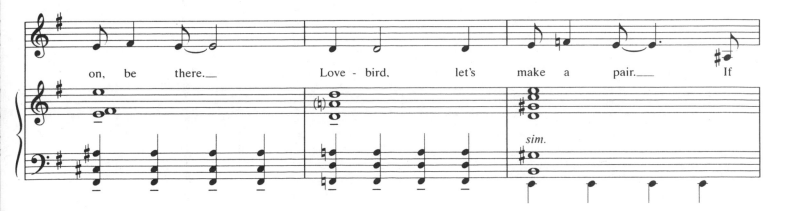

on, be there.___ Love - bird, let's make a pair.___ If

sim.

you stay a - way___ from the world I'm dream - ing of,___

cresc.

I'll be a love - bird with no one to

mf

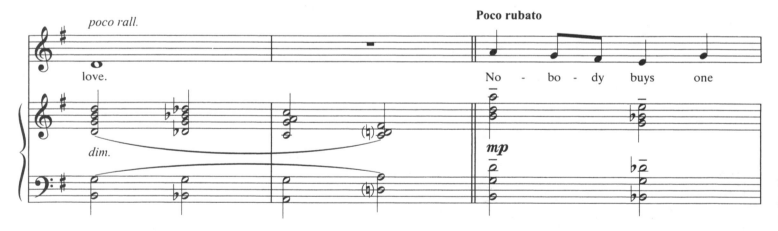

poco rall.   **Poco rubato**

love.   No - bo - dy buys one

dim.   *mp*

shoe.   No - bo - dy wants one glove.

Some things nat - u - ral - ly come with a mate. That's why I'm cry - ing

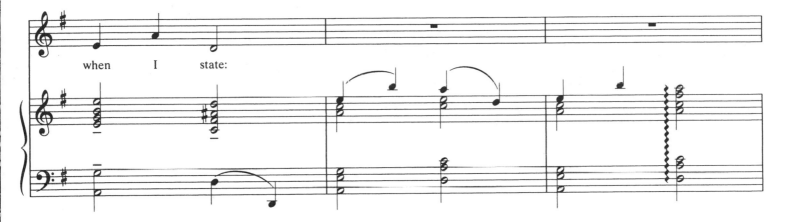

when I state:

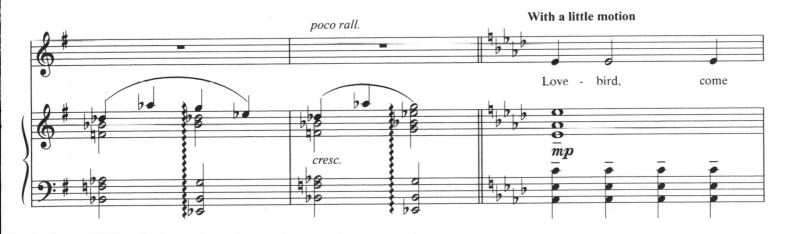

poco rall. **With a little motion**

Love - bird, come

cresc. *mp*

on, be there.___ Love - bird, let's make a pair.___ If

52

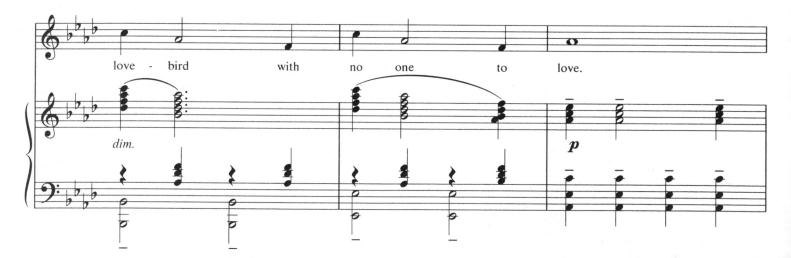

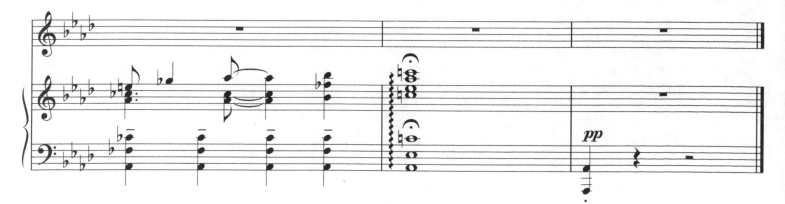

SOMEBODY OLDER

Words by FRED EBB
Music by JOHN KANDER

go - ing through now.

cresc. *dim.*

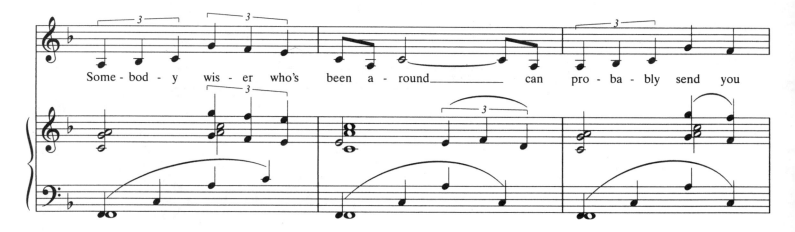

Some - bod - y wis - er who's been a - round_____ can pro - ba - bly send you

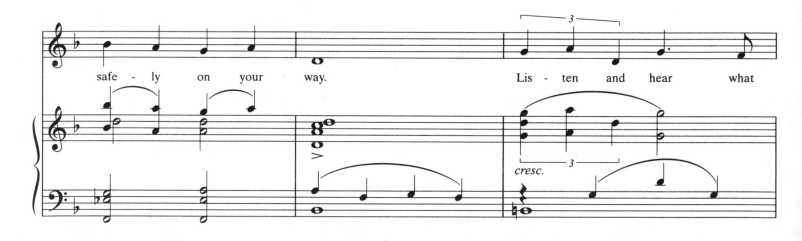

safe - ly on your way. Lis - ten and hear what

cresc.

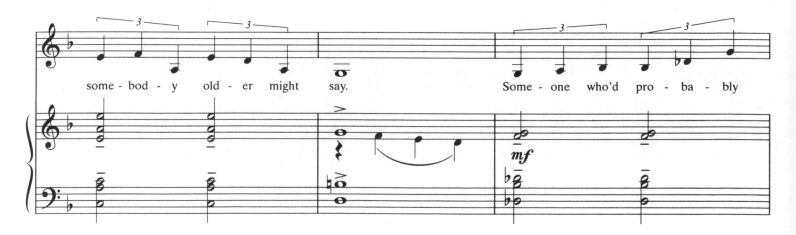

some - bod - y old - er might say. Some - one who'd pro - ba - bly

mf

be some-one a lot like me.

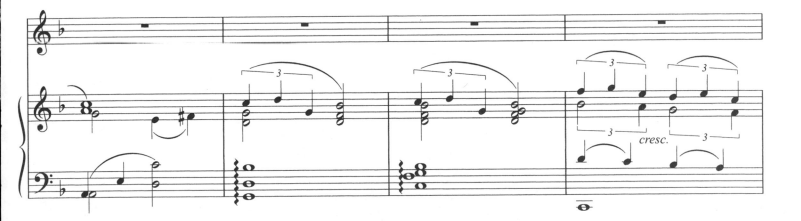

Some-bod-y wis-er who's been a-round_____ Can

56

pro - ba - bly send you safe - ly on your way. Some - bod - y young needs

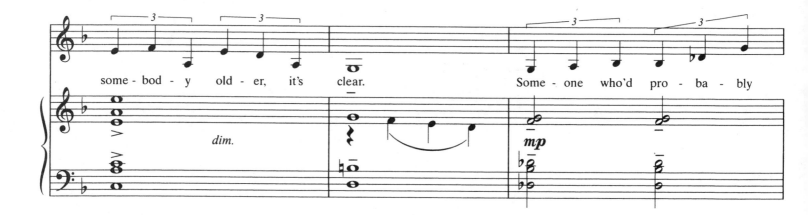

some - bod - y old - er, it's clear. Some - one who'd pro - ba - bly

cresc.
dim.
mp

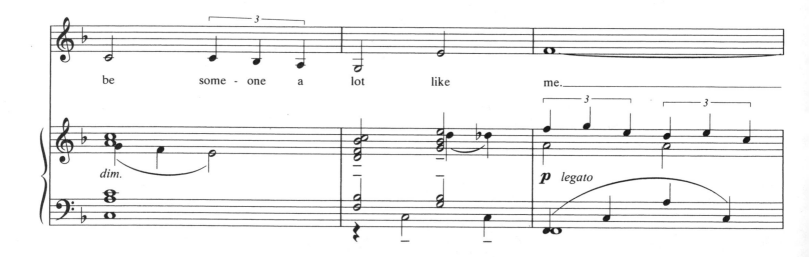

be some - one a lot like me.

dim.
p legato

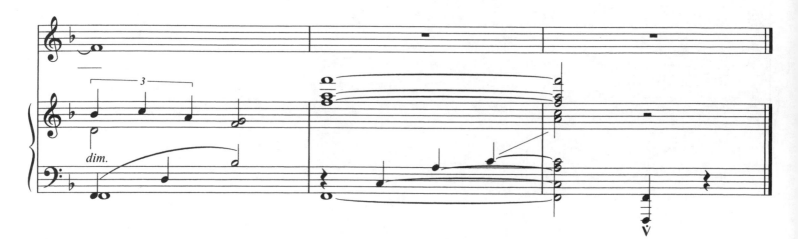

dim.

FIRST YOU DREAM

Words by FRED EBB
Music by JOHN KANDER

First you dream,_____ dream a - bout in - cred - i - ble things._____

58

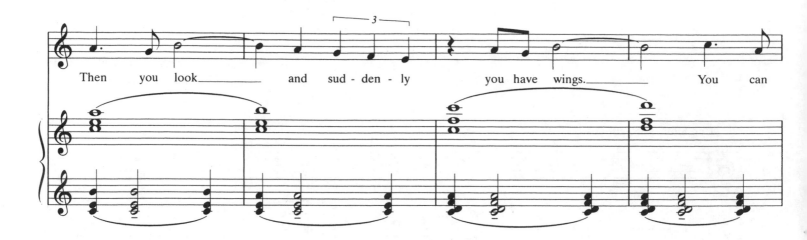

Then you look____ and sud - den - ly you have wings.____ You can

accel.

fly._____ You can fly._____ But

cresc. poco a poco

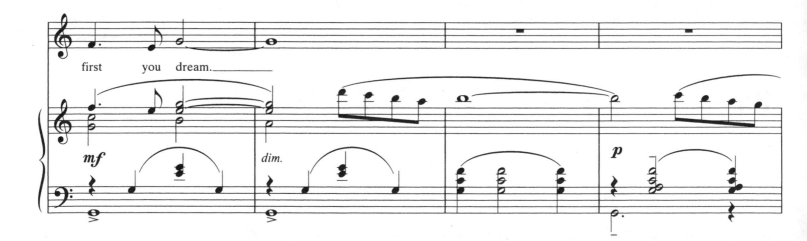

first you dream.____

mf   *dim.*   *p*

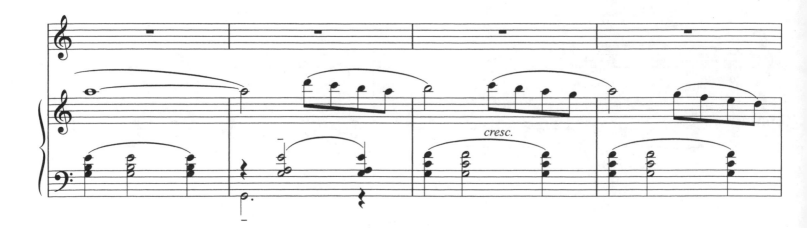

cresc.

First you dream,_____ dream a-bout re - mark-a - ble times._____

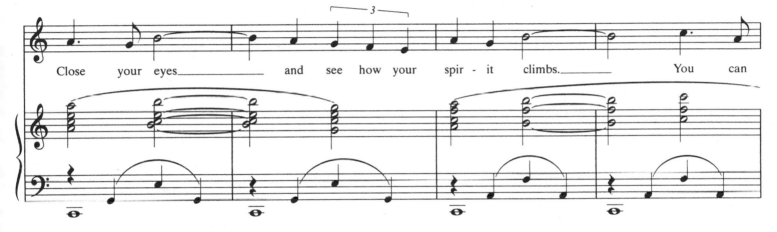

Close your eyes_____ and see how your spir - it climbs._____ You can

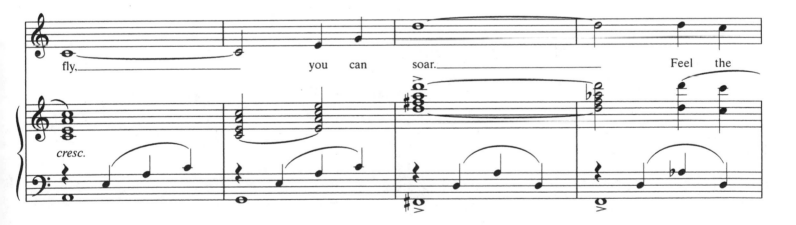

fly,_____ you can soar._____ Feel the

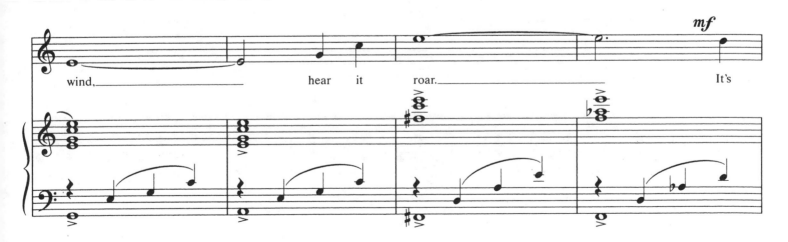

wind,_____ hear it roar._____ It's

60

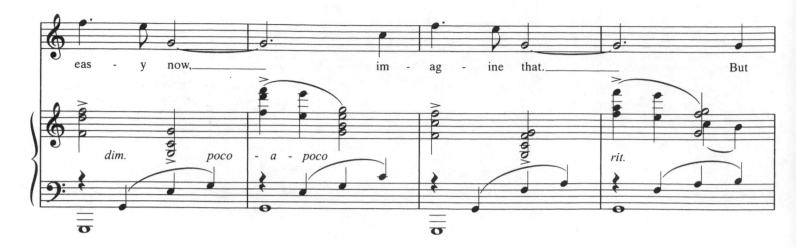

eas - y now,_____ im - ag - ine that._____ But

Slower

first you dream._____

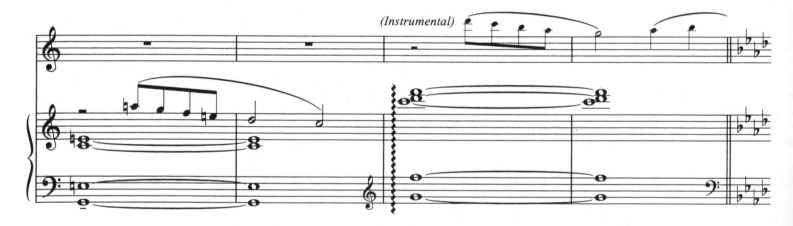

(Instrumental)

Con Moto

pp legato

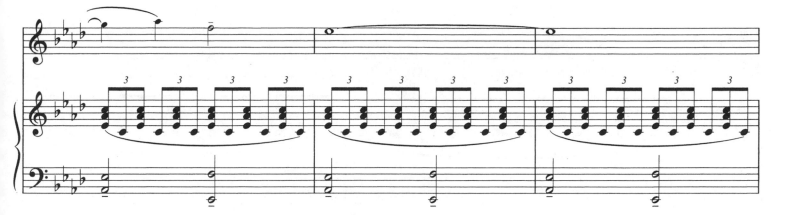

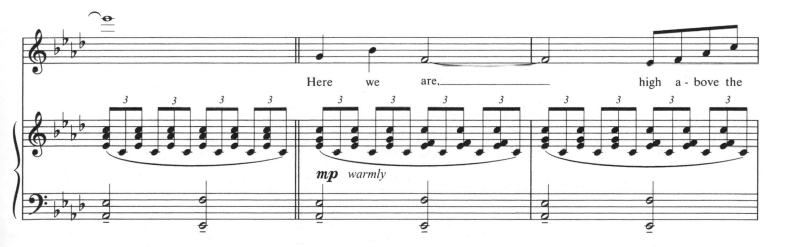

Here we are,_____ high a - bove the

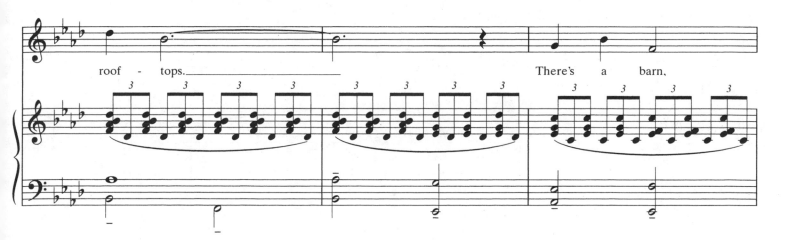

roof - tops._____ There's a barn,

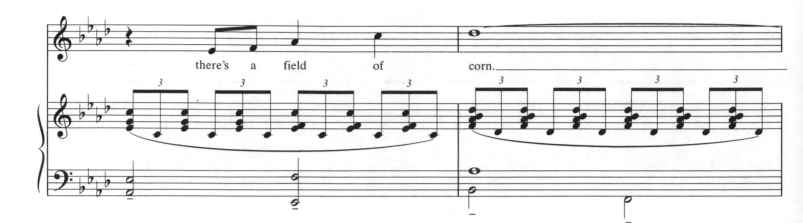

there's a field of corn.

rall. *a tempo*

And that lit - tle white house where an -

cresc. *f*

ten.

oth - er you was born. Is - n't it

dim.

fine? Is - n't it fair be - ing up

mf

to the sky._____ Straight a-

head,_____ you and I._____

To - geth - er now,_____ to -

geth - er now,_____ but first things first._____

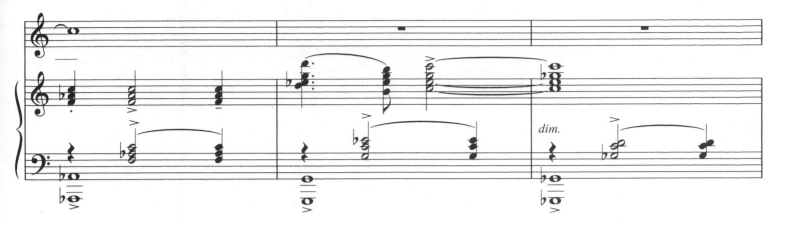

First you dream.

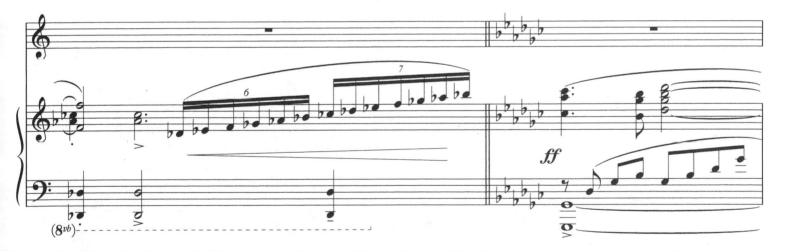

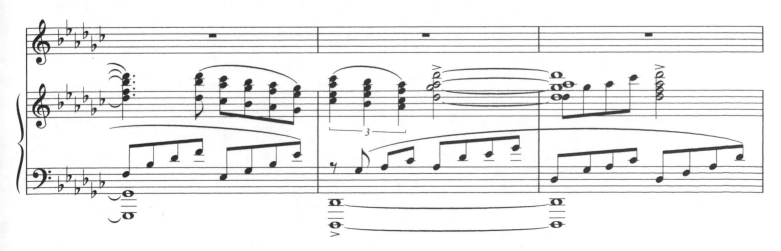

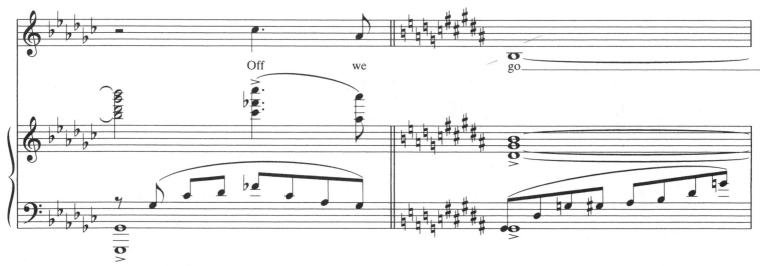

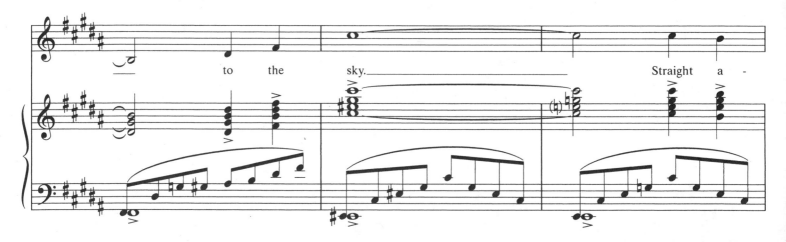

geth - er now,_____ to - geth - er now,_____

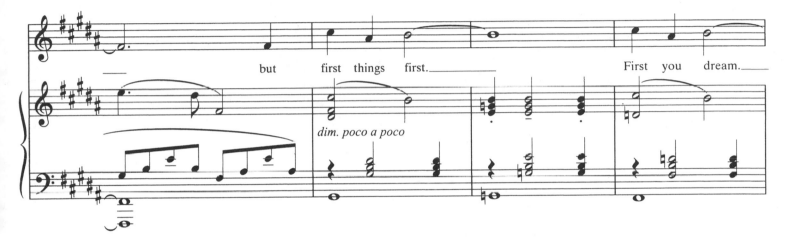

but first things first._____ First you dream._____

First you dream._____

rall. poco a poco

STEEL PIER

Words by FRED EBB
Music by JOHN KANDER

With a steady beat

Life's a par-ty. Why don't you come to the

Rub a lit - tle sun - tan lo - tion.

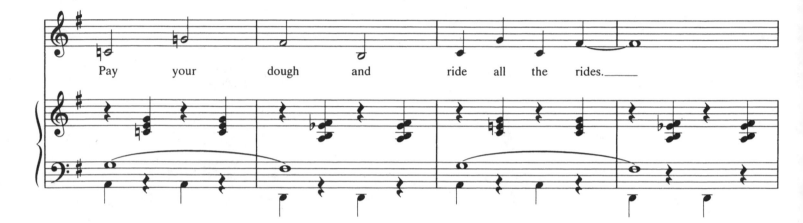

Pay your dough and ride all the rides.____

Sit on the board - walk watch - ing the tides.____

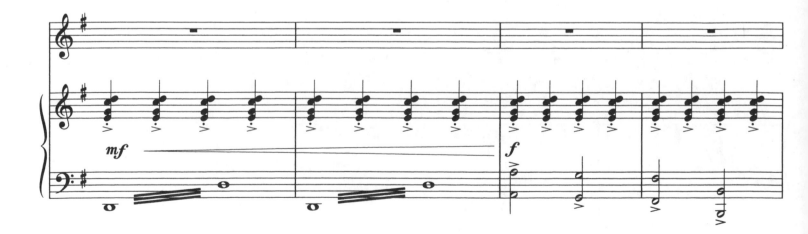

All At - lan - tic

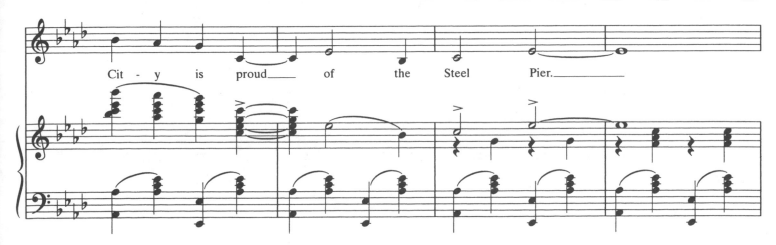

Cit - y is proud____ of the Steel Pier.____

72

No place draws a

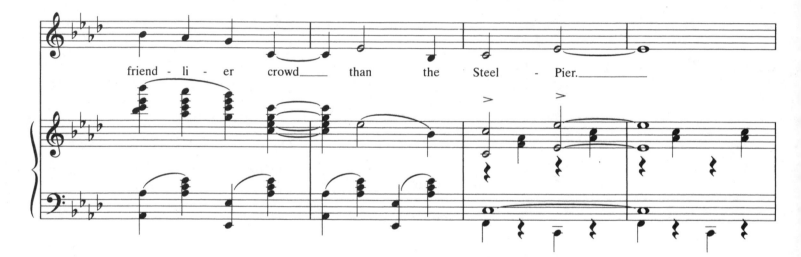

friend - li - er crowd_____ than the Steel - Pier._____

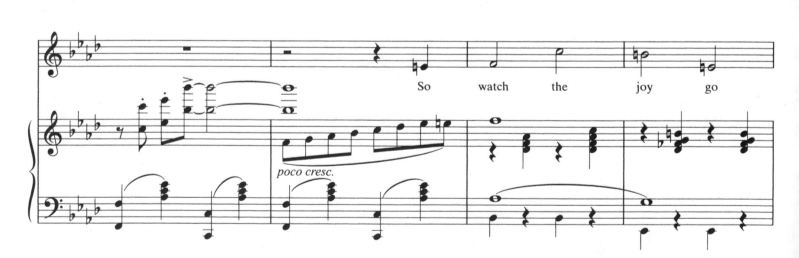

So watch the joy go

on and on,_____ like some daf - fy

ma - ra - thon._____ Bring your trou - bles here,

dim.   *mp*   *cresc. poco a poco*

watch them dis - a - pear at the tru - ly up - roar - i - ous,

f

glam - our - ous, glo - ri - ous Steel_____

Pier._____

L'istesso tempo

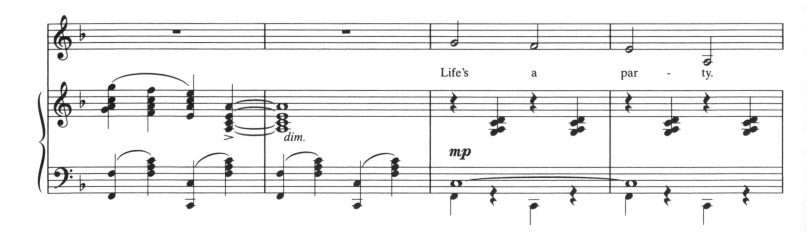

Life's a par - ty.

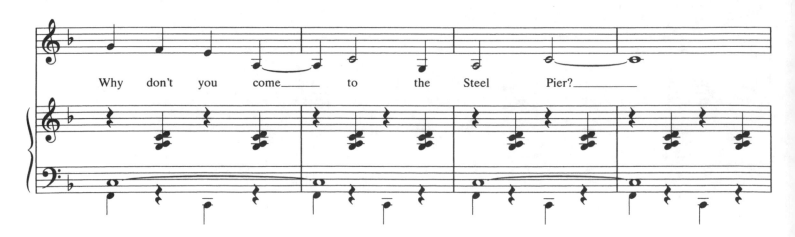

Why don't you come to the Steel Pier?

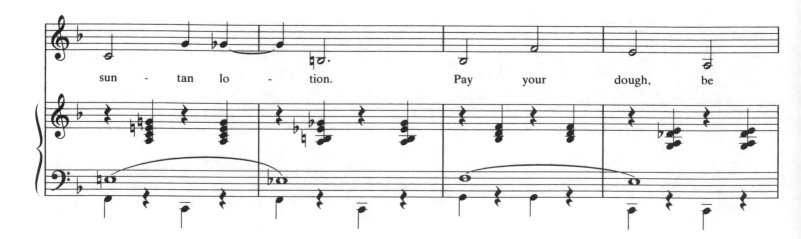

sun - tan lo - tion. Pay your dough, be

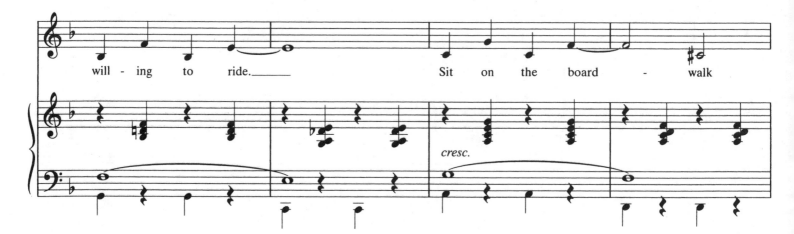

will - ing to ride._____ Sit on the board - walk

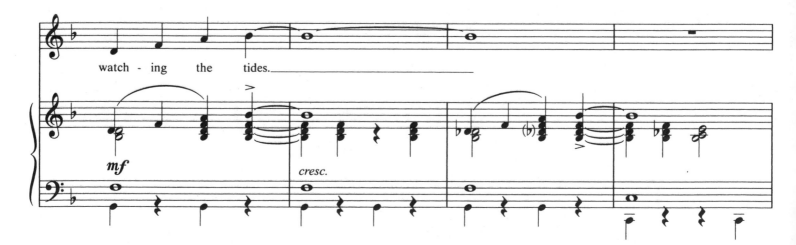

watch - ing the tides._____

All At - lan - tic Cit - y is proud___ of the

Steel Pier._____

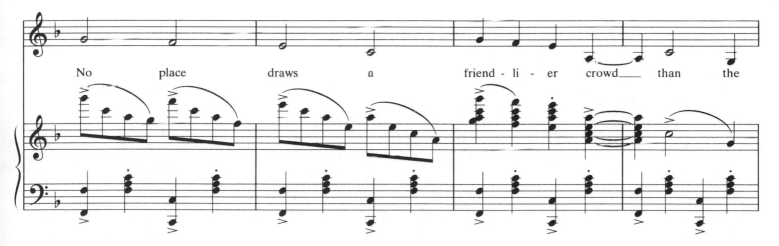

No place draws a friend - li - er crowd___ than the

Steel Pier._____ So

dim.

watch the joy go on and on,_____

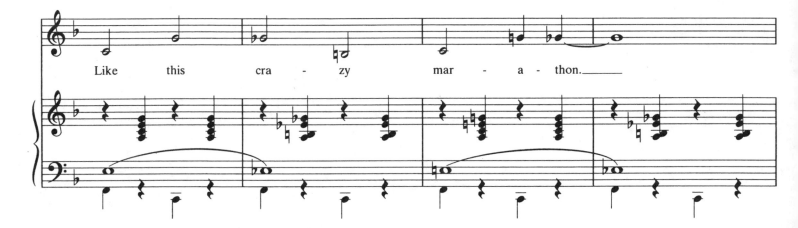

Like this cra - zy mar - a - thon._____

Bring your trou - bles here. Watch them dis - ap - pear at the

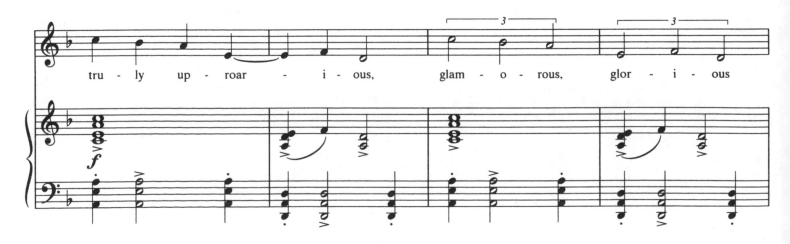

tru - ly up - roar - i - ous, glam - o - rous, glor - i - ous

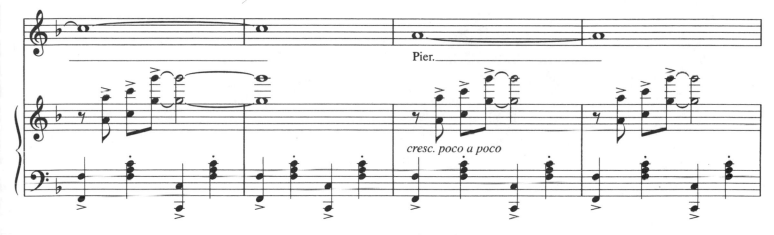

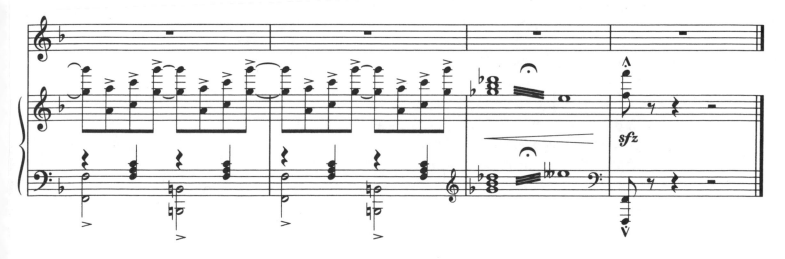

Artwork courtesy Serino Coyne

Steel Pier Logo Photography:
Ray Herbert Archives; Arnette Webster Riding Red Lipps,
photograph courtesy Arnette Webster French;
Marathon Photos from the book *Atlantic City: 125
Years of Ocean Madness* by Vicki Gold Levi and
Lee Eisenberg